THE ARABS
In the Golden Age

BY MOKHTAR MOKTEFI

Illustrated by Véronique Ageorges
Translated by Mary Kae LaRose

PEOPLES OF THE PAST

Avyx

Library of Congress Cataloging-in-Publication Data
Moktefi, Mokhtar.
[Arabes au temps de l'âge dor. English]
The Arabs in the Golden Age / by Mokhtar Moktefi : illustrated by
Véronique Ageorges ; translated by Mary Kae LaRose.
    p.   cm.—(Peoples of the past)
Translation of: Les Arabes us temps de l'âge d'or.
Summary: Describes that period when the Arabs spread their
religion, art, architecture, and great knowledge of the ancient
world throughout the Middle East and North Africa.
ISBN 978-1-887840-66-8 (pbk.)
1. Civilization, Islamic—Juvenile literature. 2. Islamic Empire—
Social life and customs—Juvenile literature. [1. Civilization,
Islamic. 2. Islamic Empire—Social life and customs.]
I. Ageorges, Véronique, ill. II. Title. III. Series: Peules du
passé. English.
DS36.85.M6513   1992
909'.97671—dc20   92-4989
                                                                            CIP
                                                                            AC

Copyright ©1991 by Editions Nathan, Paris

Originally published as Les Arabes au temps l'age d'or
(Peuples du passé series), Editions Nathan, Paris

This Edition published by Avyx, Inc. 2009

Avyx, Inc.
8032 South Grant Way
Littleton, CO 80122-2705
(303) 483-0140
E-Mail: info@avyx.com

CONTENTS

INTRODUCTION

Learning about people who live differently from us has always been interesting and important, because through understanding others we begin to see ourselves more clearly. Learning about the Arabs is not simply a matter of personal importance. It is a responsibility to all those who value peace in the world.

Much confusion about the Arab world persists in the West today. Who exactly are the Arabs? What is the relationship between the Arabic people and the Muslim religion? After all, Arabia is no longer a country. Arabs live on the Arabian Peninsula, throughout the Middle East and North Africa, and in many countries of the world today. The Islamic faith has also spread to include believers of many different races who do not speak Arabic.

And yet, this great world religion was born in what was once Arabia. And just as the foundations of the Catholic church are preserved in Latin, Arabic remains the official language of prayer and of Islamic ceremonies. It is here, in the Islamic religion, that we must look to understand who the Arabs are. Most—although not all—Arabs are Muslims.

Islam was the creative force behind the religious, military, and cultural prominence of the Arabic empire during the Golden Age, which began with the spread of the teachings of the prophet Muhammad in the early eighth century and endured roughly into the mid-thirteenth century. Decorative arts—weaving, glassmaking, tile-work, pottery, inlaid carvings in stone, plaster, and metal—had never been so beautiful. Many people, for the first time, could read. Thousands of hand-tooled, leather-bound books were filled with calligraphy so well executed that it rivaled the beauty of the miniatures accompanying the stories, poems, religious teachings, and learned treatises. Advances in technology, science, medicine, and mathematics went far beyond those made in Medieval Europe.

The common thread running through all of these contributions was Islam. It was—and is—more than a religion. It was a set of laws guiding the social, political, artistic, and moral lives of its followers. It remains a defining element of Arabic culture today.

THE ISLAMIC WORLD

The story of Arabic civilization in the Golden Age is interwoven with the spread of Islam. All the way back to prehistoric times, separate tribes of people inhabited the Arabian peninsula. Only after these distinct groups began to share a common belief in the Islamic, or Muslim, religion did they begin to call themselves both Muslims and Arabs. A single leader who ruled in the name of Allah, or God, unified the people. By the early eighth century, the Arab-Muslim empire reached all the way to Spain and across Central Asia to India. This was the beginning of the Golden Age, which would flourish for the next five hundred years.

Muhammad was the founder of Islam. He was born in Mecca, Arabia, around the year A.D. 570. His father died before he was born, and his mother passed away when he was only six years old. The young

orphan was raised by his uncle, Abu Talib, who was a poor shopkeeper. When Muhammad became a man, Abu Talib taught him everything he knew about the merchant's trade.

At the age of twenty-five, Muhammad married a wealthy widow from Mecca named Khadija. Muhammad ran his new wife's business by leading caravans in and out of Syria, where he purchased merchandise to sell in Arabia. Muhammad and Khadija had seven children, but only one of them, a girl named Fatima, lived to reach adulthood. Fatima married Ali, the son of Abu Talib.

MUHAMMAD THE PROPHET

Muhammad often went off alone to meditate in a cave on Mount Hira, near Mecca. One night, when he was about forty years old, someone claiming to be the angel Gabriel appeared to him in his sleep. Gabriel told Muhammad that he had come with a message from God. This mysterious ap-

Islam

The word Islam means submission, or surrender, to the will of Allah, the one and only God. A person who yields to Allah's will becomes a Muslim.

pearance disturbed Muhammad and woke him from his sleep. He got up and went home wondering if he hadn't been possessed by evil spirits.

Gabriel came to visit Muhammad in his sleep several times. Each time, Muhammad would wake and listen to what he had to say. He was soon convinced that Gabriel was delivering the Word of God. Muhammad began preaching and sharing what he had heard with those around him. These divine revelations continued for twenty years until the day Muhammad died. By that time, in the eyes of his followers, Muhammad had become God's prophet, or messenger, on earth.

Hegira, the Muslim New Year

In Muhammad's time, most inhabitants of Mecca were pagans who did not believe in a single God, but who worshipped a wide variety of gods called idols. Muhammad cried out to these pagans, telling them that God was the only divine power. The people of Mecca scorned and ridiculed

The Koran

The Koran is the Muslims' holy book. Next in importance to the Muslims is the Hadith, a collection of books that records the words and actions of the Prophet Muhammad. Both the Koran and the Hadith govern the behavior of believers.

him. But a small circle of faithful believers began to follow Muhammad's teachings. This group included his wife Khadija, his cousin Ali (who would become his son-in-law), several friends, a few young people, and other acquaintances. Muhammad's community, which prayed in public, began to bother the inhabitants of Mecca. Eventually his followers found that they were no longer welcome in Mecca, and some of them fled to Ethiopia.

In 622, Muhammad himself left Mecca and sought refuge in Medina. This emigration from Mecca became known as the Hegira (*hijrah* in Arabic), the first day on the Muslim calendar. The Muslim year was made up of 12 lunar months of 29 or 30 days each, which meant that there were 354 days in a year. So, according to the

Hegira, July 2, 1992 was the Muslim New Year in the year 1413.

Muhammad's Return

While in Medina, Muhammad organized his companions and allies. He wanted relationships between people to be based not on membership in tribes and clans, but rather on equality and justice. After six years in exile, Muhammad managed to rally almost all of Arabia to his faith. When he returned to Mecca, where all the city's inhabitants had since embraced his new religion, he was welcomed as a hero. At the end of his life, Muhammad made a "farewell pilgrimage" to Mecca before dying in Medina on June 8, 632. Mecca and Medina—the two small cities where Muhammad was born and where he died—became the sacred birthplaces of Islam.

THE FIVE PILLARS OF ISLAM

The teachings of Muhammad were organized into what were called the five pillars of Islam. Muslims during the Golden Age practiced these basic beliefs and traditions throughout their lives just as they do today.

"There is no God but Allah, and Muhammad is his Prophet." This declaration, or profession of faith, was known as the *shahada.* When new believers said these words they were announcing their conversion to the Muslim religion and their membership in the Muslim community. The shahada was the first of the five pillars.

Islam's second pillar was prayer. Muslims prayed five times a day. They stopped whatever they were doing to pray at dawn, at noon, in the middle of the afternoon, at sunset, and at night. The *muezzin,* or crier, climbed to the top of the minaret to announce prayer times. In the Islamic tradition, there was no organized clergy such as the priests, ministers, or rabbis of some

other religions. Followers of Islam, for the most part, communicated directly with God.

At noon on Friday, though, believers gathered at the mosque to pray together as a community. A sermon, or *khutbah,* was given by the *imam,* the guide who led the prayers. Sometimes, the people chose someone from among themselves who was especially devout or learned to lead them in prayer. At other times, a visiting religious leader might be invited to fill this role. The chief imam was the caliph. It was he who made all final decisions about both the

Positions of Prayer

political and religious matters for the empire.

Muslims were advised to perform a ritual cleansing, or ablution, before each prayer. Hands, face, and feet had to be clean. On days of great ablutions, Muslims washed their whole body. Such cleansing was required after sexual relations and the birthing of babies.

Islam's third pillar involved the Muslims' obligation to give alms, or perform *zakat.* This charitable responsibility, or tax, was

Bismillah

This expression, which means "in the name of Allah," was the opening phrase of the Koran. Muslims often pronounced this expression out loud and it appeared at the top of all written documents.

designed to help the poor and to contribute to the cost of the community at large.

Ramadan

The forth pillar of Islam required a month of fasting. Ramadan was the name given to the ninth month of the Muslim calendar. It was during this period that the Koran, the holy book of Islam, was first revealed to Muhammad. During Ramadan adults refrained from eating and drinking from sunrise to sunset. In the evening, they broke the fast. Pious followers went to pray at the mosque while others who were less religious went to entertaining shows, cafés, and pastry shops. The month of Ramadan closed with three full days of celebration.

To Mecca

The fifth pillar of Islam involved a pilgrimage, or *hajj*, to Mecca. Every healthy Muslim with sufficient funds was required to make this journey at least once in his or her lifetime. Pilgrims were expected to wear a simple robe of white fabric so that they would all look alike. The pilgrims' identical clothing and their participation in the same

Kaaba

According to tradition, this cubic monument was built by Abraham and was designed to represent God's residence on earth. The Kaaba was regarded as the center of the Islamic world. Believers, wherever they were located, turned toward this monument when they prayed.

rituals and recitation of the same prayers reinforced the notion that all believers belonged to the same community. The pilgrimage was designed to remind believers of their duty to justice, tolerance, and love of their fellow man.

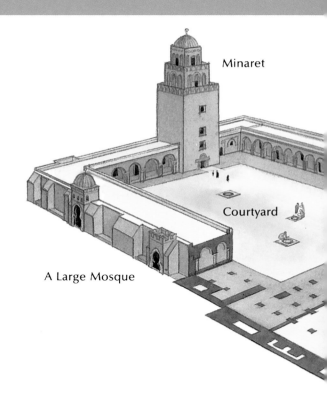

Minaret

Courtyard

A Large Mosque

THE MOSQUE

"Oh, you who are believers, when you are called to prayers on Friday, break off your business dealings and rush to call out to God. If only you knew what a good thing this would be for you," advised the Koran. It was not church bells but the chant of the muezzin, from the top of the minaret, that called the Muslims to prayer.

The mosque was the central religious building of the Islamic faith. In addition to their slender towers, or minarets, mosques often included a prayer room and an open courtyard with fountains for cleansing. Unlike churches, Muslim prayer rooms did not contain altars, statues, painted murals, or pews. In addition to the lamps and chandeliers that hung from the ceiling and the mats and carpets that covered the floor, the prayer rooms held just one piece of furniture made of stone or wood called a *minbar*. This pulpit was where all the preaching was done. A small alcove, or niche, called a *mihrab* was carved into the middle of the wall nearest to Mecca, showing worshippers where to face during their prayers.

The imam stood facing this ornately decorated alcove while he led the prayers. In principle, any Muslim adult could act as the prayer leader. Usually, though, the

faithful stood close together in rows behind the imam, where they recited the sacred prayers and bowed together in humility at the appropriate times.

The Term Mosque

The word mosque is derived from the Spanish term mezquita, *which is linked to* masdjid, *an Arab expression referring to any prayer site. The great mosque where Friday's public prayer took place was called the* djami.

Prayer room

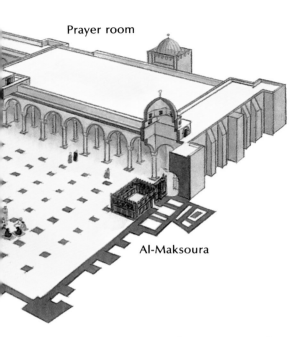

Al-Maksoura

Al-Maksoura

The Al-Maksoura was a special enclosure reserved for the sovereign within the prayer room of the city's great mosque. This alcove was usually enclosed with open latticework.

A Holy Place and Much More

Mosques were essential to both religious and cultural life. Professors often occupied part of the mosque to speak to students between prayer times. Even after special religious universities called *madrasahs* were founded, traveling scholars passing through town were free to stop at the mosque to

Muslims were expected to come to the mosque for solemn prayer at noon on Fridays. At other times and days of the week they could pray almost anywhere. In preparation for prayer, Muslims marked off a spot on the ground with a mat or carpet and turned their bodies toward Mecca. The carpet became a sacred place that allowed the believers to cut themselves off from the rest of the world. During prayers Muslims were not to think about daily concerns or about what was going on around them. They were to communicate directly with God.

give classes. Several very old universities linked to mosques, such as az-Zaytuna in Tunis, Quarawiyin in Fez, and Al-Azhar in Cairo, taught students over many centuries and are still highly respected today.

RELIGIOUS CELEBRATIONS

Muslims enjoyed festive occasions so much that they thought any religious or secular holiday was a good reason to celebrate. This was not surprising since Islam, before the arrival of western crusaders in the twelfth century, was very tolerant of other religions. Muslims at that time did not think twice about celebrating religious holidays with Christians. On Christmas Day, the whole city of Baghdad was brightly illuminated in celebration of Christ's birthday.

In Egypt, on the night of Epiphany, the Christian Feast of the Three Kings, an enormous crowd would gather on the banks of

the Nile. People ate, drank, and danced by torchlight until the sun rose.

On Palm Sunday in Jerusalem, the Muslim governor of the city accompanied the Christian procession all the way to the Church of the Resurrection. On Easter Sunday in Baghdad, Christians and Muslims paraded together in the streets before entering the Armenian monastery of Samalu, where they danced in wild abandon.

In the same way, people of all religious denominations celebrated the Iranian New Year. On this holiday, which was celebrated in the spring, it was the tradition for men and women to spray one another with perfume and to throw oranges, lemons, and bouquets of flowers at one another. Sometimes the festival looked more like a car-

nival because people danced, sang, and wore brightly colored costumes. Children received terra-cotta or glazed earthenware toys in the shape of horses, bulls, or giraffes.

Families also held private ceremonies at births, circumcisions, and weddings. The most important occasion of all was a child's memorization of the Koran. Family and friends gathered around the student and Koran teacher and offered them gifts.

Muslim Holidays

Two of the most important religious holidays for Muslims, *Id al-Fitr* and *Id al-Adha*, each lasted for three days. Id al-Fitr marked the end of the month of Ramadan. On the eve of this important celebration, city streets and mosques were brightly illuminated and fireworks were sent flying high into the sky while women finished preparing cakes and sweets. The next day, Muslims put on their best clothing. After the morning prayer at the mosque, people hugged one another,

Abraham

Abraham was a biblical prophet whom the Koran and Muslims referred to as Ibrahim al Khali, meaning "friend of God." Through his son Ishmael, Abraham was the father of Arabs and the founder of the Kaaba in Mecca. The Jews are descendents of Abraham's other son, Isaac. God tested Abraham's faith by asking him to slaughter one of his sons. The patriarch was ready to obey God's order when an angel appeared and substituted a sheep in the son's place.

to Mecca. Muslims remembered the ancient story about the test God put to Abraham by asking that he sacrifice his son. Wealthy families slaughtered lambs and gave half the meat to the poor. In addition to lamb, it was traditional to eat lots of cakes and desserts. The city streets and squares overflowed with people, activity, and entertainment.

Mawlid an-Nabin, marking the birthday of the prophet Muhammad, became a popular holiday in the twelfth century. There were also ceremonies mourning the death of Muhammad's grandson Husain and celebrations on the birthday of Fatima, Muhammad's daughter.

exchanged wishes of goodwill, and went to visit friends and relatives. Children stuffed themselves with candy.

For three whole days the streets bustled with activity and noise. Tightrope artists, magicians, bear leaders, marionettists, snake charmers, storytellers, minstrels, and musicians all added to the festivities.

Id al-Adha, the holiday of sacrifice, always fell on the last day of the pilgrimage

THE RULE OF THE CALIPH

During his lifetime, Muhammad's religious leadership had begun to transform the Arabs from a group of tribes into a single people. But when he died in 632, Muhammad had not yet chosen a successor. His companions decided to elect a caliph, or *khalifah*, from among themselves. The caliph was not a prophet, nor did he possess a prophet's power. His role was to lead the community according to the principles of the Koran and the life of Muhammad.

The first four caliphs were modest men who were likable and easy to approach. But those men who later came to hold this position were more powerful and remote than these early leaders had been. The caliphate became a hereditary title that was passed on through a royal family from father to son or, on occasion, from brother to brother. Until the tenth century, one supreme caliph ruled. From this time on, other Muslim leaders claimed the titles. These rivals included the Fatimids in Egypt, the Umayyad in Muslim Spain, and the Almoravids and their successors in North Africa and Spain.

The Caliph Holds Court

The simple traditions of the early caliphs came to be replaced by the protocol, or set conventions, of sumptuous palace life. Ceremonies marking the appointment of important government officials and receptions for foreign ambassadors were run according to rigid guidelines. The caliph, who presided over such ceremonies, sat with his legs crossed on a *sarir*, or bed-shaped throne, which was decorated with cushions and silk and topped with a canopy.

The chamberlain, or chief of protocol, would announce each member of the court and seat him according to his rank. The prince and the sons of the caliph were announced first. They were followed by both the vizier and the military commander in chief. These men would kiss the monarch's hand and the ground at his feet before taking their places to his right and his left. After an impressive silence, the high-ranking dignitaries entered according to their order of importance. They greeted the sovereign by kissing the edge of the carpet. Officers and soldiers would stand behind the ropes, leaving the center of the room empty. After all these people had taken their places, the chamberlain introduced the important person to whom the caliph had granted an audience.

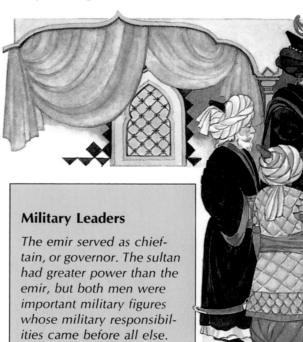

Military Leaders

The emir served as chieftain, or governor. The sultan had greater power than the emir, but both men were important military figures whose military responsibilities came before all else.

As head of the armed forces, the caliph's role was to defend his people against "infidels," those who attacked or tried to corrupt the Islamic religion. The caliph often traveled through the countryside to secure his borders and to take care of important government affairs. Key members of his court always accompanied him. When he returned home to his palace in the city, great welcome festivities were planned. The entire town would break out in joyful celebration, as crowds spilled into the brightly lit city streets.

A Magnificent Gift

When caliph Harun al-Rashid presented an elephant as a gift to Charlemagne, king of the Franks, the people of Aachen organized a triumphant welcome for the elephant.

The Royal Pilgrimage

The caliph, who was also called *Emir al Mouminine,* or leader of the faithful, was expected to make a pilgrimage to Mecca every year. During his journey he demonstrated his generosity by giving alms to the poor. He would also often command that shelters, mosques, fountains, and wells be built along the roads heavily traveled by pilgrims.

But this journey to Mecca, in addition to the military campaigns, was tiring. For this reason, some caliphs did not actually make the pilgrimage themselves, but entrusted this task to their closest associates.

The Vizier

The honorific title of vizier was given to the caliph's closest counselor and associate. The same term was also used to refer to government ministers.

A VISIT TO THE PALACE OF BAGHDAD

Someone, most likely in the service of the caliph, described the following preparations for the splendid reception given in 917 by the caliph of Baghdad for the Byzantine ambassadors: "The vizier ordered all men in possession of a complete set of armor to assemble in the rooms, corridors, and secret passages of the palace. He commanded that all the buildings be covered with carpet and completely decorated."

A Dazzling Entrance

Guests arriving at the palace discovered that it had been covered with silk draperies and carpets. In the great stable they passed through a corridor made up of two rows of three hundred splendid horses fitted with gold and silver saddles or large silk covers. Before reaching the palace, the visitors strolled through a pen containing wild animals and viewed four elephants and two giraffes. They passed by one hundred lions, each attached to a leash held by a trainer, standing in two neat rows. In the new palace situated between the gardens they came upon a mercury lake, brighter than polished silver, in which four gilded boats were floating.

The Byzantine guests went from one sumptuous palace to another before entering the most beautiful building of all where the caliph was waiting for them. During the audience that he granted to the Byzantines, at the caliph's command, an in-

genious contraption made a large tree of gold and silver spring from the ground. On the branches of the magical tree were songbirds made of precious metal. The palace fountains flowed with musk and rose water.

their culture, their elegant clothing, and the singular way in which they draped their hair in an upside-down "V" over their foreheads.

The palace was a place of unimaginable luxury. Men and women alike competed to determine who wore the most elegant clothing. Inhabitants of the palace wore brocade clothing decorated with precious gems and jewels. In the winter, parties and receptions were held within the palace itself. In warmer seasons they were held in royal gardens that could be illuminated at night. Musicians, minstrels, and dancers provided lively entertainment. Perfume radiating from flowers, and incense burners added to the enchantment.

Elegant boating parties were held on the river in Baghdad. Beautifully decorated small boats filled with musicians and singers sailed on the Tigris. Some of these small craft were shaped like lions and horses; others resembled elephants and eagles. Still others were made to look like dolphins and snakes.

Life in the Palace

The sovereign's large residence was an impressive, almost magical sort of small town within the city limits of Baghdad. In addition to private living quarters, the residence contained reception rooms, gardens, and many offices where government business was conducted.

A large number of *kouttab,* or secretaries, several of whom were women, worked busily within these offices. Letters had to be finalized, and files required preparation and updating. The skilled bureaucrats stood out among ordinary citizens because of

Privileged Companions

The nadim, *who served as artists, scholars, and men of letters, were the privileged companions of the caliph. Their job was to amuse the sovereign with activities such as literary debates and chess games.*

WARRIORS OF ISLAM

"It is written that when the Prophet Muhammad had completed a military campaign he said, "We have just returned from a little *jihad* in order to embark upon the important *jihad*, which is the work of the soul."

Here, Muhammad describes two meanings for *jihad*. The first meaning is "the work of the soul," or the lifelong effort that all people must make to improve themselves by struggling against pride, selfishness, and weakness. The other meaning, that of "a holy war," is the one that is most commonly used today.

After Muhammad's death, when the caliphs took charge, they began to battle to expand the boundaries of the Islamic world. Within only a hundred years their empire stretched all the way from northern Spain to India. The word *jihad* describes the wars that were fought in the name of Allah to spread the teachings of Muhammad.

Not all Muslims were Arabs

The cavalrymen and the camel drivers who left Arabia to spread the new religion were eager and skillful fighters. In the name of the calif and of Allah they conquered an enormous empire. It wasn't very long before Syrians, inhabitants from the Maghreb (North Africans), Iranians, and Afghans had joined the Muslim army. In some regions, non-Arab Muslims who had converted to Islam made up the largest portion of the troops. Non-Muslims also joined the army in order to avoid paying taxes and to receive a share of the booty won in battle.

These early warriors were eventually replaced by professional soldiers. Turks gave cavalrymen an important competitive ad-

vantage by teaching them how to shoot with a bow and arrow while riding on galloping horses.

Secret Weapons

Little by little, Arabs perfected elaborate military equipment that allowed them to better lay siege to enemy cities and towns. They developed military tricks, weapons, and movable shelters. The marines and the land army used *naffatun* troops, or special forces, which hurled at the enemy a colorless flammable liquid called naphtha. This crude petroleum was propelled through a long hose, the forerunner of a flamethrower. Soldiers used javelins and arrows

whose tips were filled with flammable naphtha and iron filings. In face-to-face combat, they blinded the enemy with powerful syringes filled with vitriol and acid.

The research, development, and testing of these chemical weapons was kept top

Ribats

Small forts, called ribats had tall lookout towers. They gave shelter to believers who had volunteered to help defend Arab territory. These forts lined the borders and the coasts open to attack or invasion by foreigners. Rabat, the current capital city of Morocco, is the site of an old ribat.

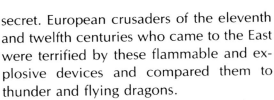

secret. European crusaders of the eleventh and twelfth centuries who came to the East were terrified by these flammable and explosive devices and compared them to thunder and flying dragons.

One of the Arabs' most effective military tricks was to dress cavalrymen and horses in non-flammable fabric. This special material allowed them to wear helmets equipped with naphtha flares without risk of burning their skin. At night, just before entering the enemy camp, the soldiers lit

War Manuals

Army officers and technicians read many books to learn the techniques of war. For example, it was through reading war manuals that they learned how to lay siege to a city. These books also explained how to operate military machines and weapons.

the flares on their armor. The very sight of these oncoming "fire monsters" surprised and terrified the enemy. Men and horses fled in all directions.

TRAVEL THROUGH THE EMPIRE

The ancient Arab world contained many large expanses of sand and rock—the Sahara in North Africa, the deserts of the Arabian Peninsula, and those of Asia to the northeast. Such terrain meant that every traveler making an overland journey had to cross a wide expanse of desert. Nobody who embarked on such a dangerous adventure ever did so without risking death by thirst, exposure, or exhaustion. This explains why all voyages were made in groups, or caravans.

The Bedouins were excellent guides and herdsmen. They knew how to navigate across the flat, infertile steppes without any navigational instruments whatsoever. Their vast knowledge encompassed not only animals but stones, winds, and plants. Merchants transporting goods and travelers of all kinds found that Bedouins were indispensable guides and caravaneers.

THE CARAVAN

Several dozen camels usually made up a caravan, but sometimes hundreds of them traveled together. Once in a rare while, caravans with five or six thousand camels passed by! When caravans grew to be this large, it appeared as if the whole world were in motion. The caravan's collective

Dromedaries, or one-humped camels nicknamed "desert vessels," were ideally suited to this climate. Bedouins, or nomadic Arabs, raised large herds of a thousand or more dromedaries.

Crossing Rivers

Sometimes caravans rode across rivers on rafts made of inflatable wineskins (bags made from the skins of animals). Or they crossed navigable rivers on bridges made of boats lined up one next to the other. Of course, there were also many bridges made of stone.

ranged ahead of time with the heads of local tribes who would grant safe-conduct passes to the convoy or have it accompanied by designated tribe members.

movements, such as departures, rest stops, and the setting up and taking down of tents, were announced by drum rolls. Overland journeys usually lasted several months. Since each camel could carry a load weighing over 220 pounds (100 kilos), caravans were able to transport as much cargo as would fit into a very large ship. Wealthy merchants, important people, and women rode in palanquins, enclosed couches with shafts that rested on the camels' backs.

Traveling in caravans was not always safe. At certain points throughout history it was risky to travel by caravan in some regions of the Arab world. Wars and local revolts disturbed the long-distance trade that caravans made possible. In the ninth century, for example, serious trouble in China interrupted the overland trade of silk. On the other hand, the crusades, which began in the eleventh century, greatly contributed to the exchange of goods between merchants in French and Arab territories.

Caravans always traveled with escorts hired to protect against attacks by bandits or wild beasts. In some cases, journeys through unfriendly territory had to be ar-

Were There Roads?

Chariots and carts were not well suited for travel in the steppes and across the desert. But camels could travel just about anywhere without difficulty and could reach places where there were no roads. There were often paths carved into the mountainsides to make their journey easier.

TRAVELING FAR

"Go far and wide in search of your subsistence. If you do not find great wealth, you will have nourished your mind and your spirit." The Arab author of the *Book of Countries* shared this wisdom with his compatriots in the year 896.

In the tenth century, the *dar al Islam,* as Arab territory was called, extended from the borders of China to Spain, from the coast of the Caspian Sea in Russia all the way to southeastern France and central Africa. People, products, and ideas circulated back and forth within this vast region. Each year tens of thousands of people came to Mecca. Arabs were always traveling the roads, rivers, and seas of their known world. But they never ventured beyond its borders into South Africa or into northern or eastern Europe.

Merchants Buying and Selling

Merchants traded many luxury products— silk, porcelain, pearls, precious stones, coral, ivory, furs, and perfume. They also bought and sold wood, iron, pewter, mercury, gold, and silver. Some merchants purchased their goods with sacks full of gold and silver coins. Others used more modern forms of payment such as letters of credit and *chakk,* or checks.

Travel by Boat

How would Arab merchants ever have been able to travel to the farthest outreaches of the empire without boats? Arabs traveled frequently to Asia to trade at the ports of Vietnam and Ceylon. Some who had come to know the Orient even chose to set up shop and live in the Cantonese province of China. Large Chinese junks laden with goods came to trade at the ports of the Persian Gulf.

Arab navigators knew how to use the monsoon winds to their advantage. On their return trip from India, they sailed with the wind lashing behind them directly toward Arabia or East Africa. Passengers and goods also traveled frequently down navigable rivers, and Arab sailors were not afraid to hoist their sails out in the great expanse of the Mediterranean Sea.

Ports, beacons, and lighthouses stretched along the coasts of the Arab world. However, despite all this protection, Indian pirates riding in swift rowboats sometimes managed to attack the Arabs' slow, heavy sailboats.

A Caravansary

Customs

When boats and caravans arrived in ports or cities of a foreign country they had to go through a customs check. Customs officers recorded the name, country of origin, and a brief description of each passenger. They levied taxes on all transported goods.

Other Arab ships equipped with large sails could transport over a thousand passengers. These large ships contained as many as a hundred sleeping compartments and were equipped with shops for snacks and refreshments, a laundry, and even a hair salon.

Caravansaries

Caravansaries, or inns designed to accommodate caravans, welcomed travelers and their goods all over the Arab world. Sometimes caravansaries were large buildings whose single entrance opened onto a courtyard with a drinking trough and a fountain. Offices, guard posts, stables, and shops were located around the courtyard on the first floor. Communal sleeping rooms were located on the first floor. Large caravansaries served as wholesale markets where retailers and shop owners came to purchase their wares.

Often there was a mosque in these large complexes, and attached to the mosque was a *hamman,* or bathhouse. Public baths were popular among Muslims for ceremonial ablutions and health reasons as well as for fun. Steam rose from a jet of hot water that was piped up into a basin in the central, domed room of the hamman. In the cooler, outer rooms, people relaxed with drinks and chatter.

A POSTAL SYSTEM

Al barid means post office. This remarkable government organization had branches in all the Arab territories and succeeded in delivering mail from one end of the empire to the other. Cavalrymen and *meharists* (soldiers mounted on camels) traveled night and day over countless postal routes.

Mailmen on horseback traveled straight through rough, hilly regions in order to shorten their journey. The need for speedy delivery of news and information even led to the development of airmail. Carrier pigeons and light signals were fast ways to communicate short messages.

Airmail

Thousands of pigeons, each bearing the sovereign's insignia on its beak or foot, flew directly from one post office to another. The letters they carried, just like the airmail letters we send today, were written on lightweight paper and folded in a special way. The pigeons were set free from post office towers or terraces. There were many post offices in the postal network, and the carrier pigeons were able to carry mail to places the regular postal service couldn't reach.

Only the army had the right to send light signal messages. This secret communications code was used to signal attacks along the coast or on national borders. Light signals were transmitted from the tall lookout towers of the ribat or from one post office terrace or look-out tower to the next. These light signals, made of fire or smoke could travel thousands of miles within a twenty-four-hour period.

Mailing Letters

All mail had to be brought directly to the post office where a postal employee would record the letter or package in a register before sending it. Postage was paid upon delivery by the person receiving the letter.

Post Offices in the Arab World

Over nine hundred post offices lined the great communications routes of the Arab empire! They were spaced at intervals of 12.5 to 25 miles (20 to 40 kilometers). Some post offices were located within the caravansaries, but most of them were independent buildings that provided shelter for a few horses and several guards. Post offices were typically built around open courtyards and were equipped with living quarters, a mosque, stables, a store, a water tank, and latrines. The tower from which light signals were sent rose from the outer corner of this building.

Top Secret Mail

Al amana, or mail, was regarded by Arabs as a sacred trust that had to be delivered to its destination intact. Transporting a letter was considered a mission of confidence and trust. Government officials and ordinary citizens alike sealed their letters with wax and a personal stamp. Engravers recorded the imprints and the names of those to whom they sold seals in large registers.

CITY AND COUNTRY LIFE

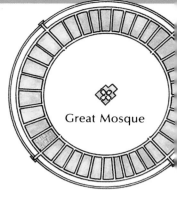

Plan for Baghdad

Great Mosque

At a time when very few urban areas in Europe had as many as ten thousand inhabitants, the Arab world was sprinkled with many very large cities. In the tenth century, roughly fifteen *amsar,* or capital cities, housed hundreds of thousands of citizens.

Some Arab cities popped up like mushrooms in places where there had been no previous development at all. Others grew out of old town centers. Some of these cities were gigantic. In Iraq, Samarra spread

out over 22 miles (35 kilometers). One of its great mosques was 1,444 feet (440 meters) long and its minaret was 164 feet (50 meters) tall. The four laps of the track at the racecourse stretched out over 7 miles (11 kilometers).

From a distance, the ten-story buildings in the Egyptian city of Cairo looked like mountains. In Spain, Cordova sheltered more than half a million people, while the population of Iraq's Baghdad was roughly two million.

City Planning

The caliph who founded Baghdad drew the plans for the new circle-shaped city himself. The royal palace and the mosque were in the center of the circle. They were surrounded by an open expanse dotted with gardens and housing for the many members of the royal following. Encircling the city, just inside the protective exterior wall, were the houses of the people. The only ways to enter the fortified city were through four heavily guarded gates.

One hundred thousand people worked at building the city of Baghdad for four long years until, in 762, they completed their gigantic task.

In the center of every Arab city there was a mosque. Wide, straight boulevards filled with outdoor markets extended outward from the mosque. Capital cities housed the palaces of the sovereign as well as those

Taking the Doors

Many Arabs had to count their pennies. Some dishonest tenants were even tempted to take the doors and parts of the roof from their former homes when they moved because wood was so expensive.

belonging to provincial leaders and governors. Citadels, or fortresses, and ramparts surrounded the city to protect it from hostile invasion. Caravansaries, hammams, and hospitals were other important public buildings of the city.

Most of these buildings were constructed with bricks made of dried mud that had been coated with lime or plaster. Plaster was an especially decorative choice because it could be sculpted or painted. Architectural ornamentation in Arab cities was made of colorful ceramic tiles. Masons also built with stone when they could find it. Marble, granite, onyx, and rare woods were sometimes imported from faraway lands for the construction of palaces and beautiful residences.

Comfortable Housing

Houses were generally built around open courtyards onto which the windows and

doors of the first floor opened. A staircase inside the house led to a terrace on the roof. Wealthy residents often had patios with pools and decorative fountains. In the

summer, residents escaped from the heat by retiring into the house's underground rooms. Basements of Arab houses were filled with luxurious carpets, wall hangings, comfortable chairs and couches with silk cushions. Chests and jewelry boxes made of wood and metal were placed around the rooms. Beautifully decorated niches were carved out here and there from the walls.

In the evening, candles, candelabras, oil lamps made of terra-cotta, and glass lamps hanging from the ceiling provided lots of light. Residents enjoyed cool, fresh air in the gardens, which were closed off from the neighbor's property by a wall. Palm,

Water Merchants

In the hot streets of Cairo men carried goatskins filled with water around their necks. They sold this water to thirsty passersby, who drank it through straws made of linen.

orange, and other kinds of trees grew in the garden alongside flowers such as roses, jasmine, carnations, and lilacs.

Large houses contained their own hammam. Baked clay or lead pipes carried water to different parts of the city. In Cairo, water from the Nile was transported in goatskins or cowhides on the backs of donkeys, camels, or men.

Law and Order

Baghdad, which covered 40 square miles (100 square kilometers), was the world's largest city. Big cities such as Damascus, Cairo, Qayrawan (in North Africa), and Cordova attracted all kinds of people. Homeless beggars wandered the streets looking for a job and a place to live. From time to time, misery and poverty caused

riots where people plundered houses and shops and set buildings on fire. Gangs armed with heavy sticks and large shields made of palm leaves confronted the mounted police force.

The police, or *shurtah,* were responsible for maintaining order. Policemen patrolled the city both night and day. In Baghdad, their leader, the prefect of police, was a

very important person who was close to the caliph. The police force was responsible for carrying out the punishments decided upon by the judge, or *qadi.* Policemen were even allowed to inflict corporal punishment. The police held so much power that sometimes they abused it and punished citizens unjustly.

TO MARKET, TO MARKET!

Al Yakoubi, a ninth century geographer, described the *souk,* or bazaar, of Baghdad in the following way: "The souk was a large market, 12 kilometers [7.5 miles] long, and 6 kilometers [almost 4 miles] wide. Each trade was assigned specific avenues within the bazaar so that people from different professions and walks of life didn't have to mingle with each other."

He was a very good observer. The souk, usually located near the great mosque, was a place where people from all over the city came together to buy and sell. While these markets may have looked as if they were overflowing with crowds and products of all sorts, they were not at all disorganized.

In fact, town markets were designed and built according to careful, strict plans. The long, wide avenues of the market were covered with vaulted wooden ceilings or branches. Boutiques and booths of the same size lined both sides of the passageways. At the end of the day, merchants simply closed the top and bottom shutters, which served as canopies and display tables while the shops were open.

Markets for luxury goods such as jewels and fine fabrics were located in closed buildings or in the protected areas around the mosque. Fruits and vegetables, on the other hand, were sold near the city gates on the periphery of the marketplace so that the market farmers would not block traffic with their produce-laden camels and mules. Smaller souks in residential quarters of the city allowed inhabitants to do their daily shopping close to home.

Markets were organized according to types of products sold by members of a guild, or association of merchants. This grouping of similar items allowed shoppers to compare the products and prices and benefit from the competition between the vendors. The fact that all goods of the same kind were located in one place also made it easier for the *muhtasib,* the chief of municipal police, and his agents to survey and inspect goods.

These agents, who were selected for their honesty and competence, were responsible for watching over the craftsmen and merchants in the marketplace. They conducted regular inspections to ensure that products were of good quality and that the prices were fair. After checking to make sure that weights, measures, and scales were functioning properly, the inspectors stamped them with a special mark. They also placed seals on goods produced for export.

In the Arab empire, certain behavior was against the law. For example, a man and a woman were not supposed to display their intimacy in public. A man whose beard had turned gray was forbidden to dye it black in order to appear more attractive to women. The muhtasib enforced these moral codes in the market.

He could impose penalties on people found guilty of cheating or fraud without going through a court of law. The muhtasib determined what kind of punishment guilty parties deserved; he decided when cheaters should be beaten or taken on what was called the "walk of shame." He also had the right to confiscate defective products or rigged weights and measures. If craftsmen or merchants were found guilty of cheating more than once, the muhtasib forbid them to practice their trade ever again.

Eating in the Marketplace

Arab merchants sold prepared foods in the street. Passersby were able to sample

The Walk of Shame

People found guilty of fraud were forced to make a "walk of shame" through town on a donkey. The cheaters riding through the city streets were forced to wear brightly colored hats with bells while town criers shouted out their crimes for all to hear.

eggplant or cheese dumplings and pastries as they strolled. In the cities, strollers could purchase hot, spicy sausages called *merguez.* Restaurants and rotisseries were located inside the market. Inexpensive cafés served soups thickened with flour or starch, which contained a few bits of chopped meat here and there. Rice, bean, lentil, and chick pea mash were easy to find. Bread was usually made from wheat, but in times of scarcity, it was made with barley or millet.

Also from wheat came a spicy salad called *tabbouleh.* It was simple to prepare. Bulgar, or cracked wheat, was soaked in a bowl for about fifteen minutes. Then, after draining the water off, scallions, parsley, mint, chopped tomatoes, oil, and lemon juice were added. Olives and cucumbers might also be stirred into the mixture. Tabbouleh was a common Arabian dish long before

Dirham and Dinar

The most important coins were the gold dinar, which weighed 4.25 grams, and the silver dirham, which weighed 2.95 roughly grams. In different periods the dirham was worth a tenth, a twentieth, or a thirtieth of the dinar. Money in the ancient Arab world was weighed, not counted.

this time, and it is still eaten in many parts of the world today.

Eating in Restaurants

In restaurants, people with money could order sheep or lamb. Fine Arab cuisine included stew, fried vegetable dumplings, meatball skewers, and chopped vegetables. Chicken, squab, partridges, and other poultry were also available to those who could afford it. Arab chefs used lots of herbs, spices, and onions.

Delicious fruits and cakes were served for dessert. Most pastries were made with honey, almonds, pitted dates, walnuts, or crushed pine kernels. They were flavored with cinnamon, orange blossoms, and musk.

Milk was the most popular beverage. However, there were also many fruit juices and cordials.

SPECIAL WARES

In the very heart of the city, next to the great mosque, jewelers strung pearls, set precious stones—diamonds, sapphires, emeralds, and rubies—and molded and hammered silver and gold. Sweet, subtle odors drew strollers to the outer edges of the market where perfume was sold.

In the perfume market, merchants sold perfumes made with roses, violets, lemons, orange blossoms, and musk. They also offered soaps, creams, hair-removing lotions, and henna for hair coloring. Nearby, in the fabric souk, shoppers looked at striped cloth, brushed velvet fabrics, and material trimmed with fringe.

Weaving cloth on a loom was a highly developed art. Materials for clothing, wall-hangings, coverings, and even tents were often woven with silk threads. Many of the designs for these fabrics came from pre-Islamic Persia.

Craftsmen at Work

At the far end of the market's main avenue, at the suq's outer limits, there were extraordinary things to see. Coppersmiths, cobblers, tailors, saddlers, and wrought-iron craftsmen made their products as shoppers looked on. Their boutiques served as workshops. Craftsmen at the market sold their goods both wholesale and retail.

Rug merchants spread out beautiful carpets in the street for everyone to walk on. This was their way of giving their clients a royal welcome. Rugs were an important feature in the Arab world. People traditionally sat and slept on them. The tremendous skill of carpet weavers, who wove beautiful

figures and designs into wool and even silk carpets, turned rugs into works of art.

At the Outskirts of Town

Those who produced pottery, tiles, and bricks needed water and lots of working space. Raw materials, tile kilns, and containers of combustible fuel were found be-

yond the city limits near rivers or watering holes. All the elements of the "polluting" trades, such as the glassworkers' ovens and the tanners' vats, were found on the outskirts of town as well.

Ceramic arts and glassmaking flourished in the Golden Age. Glazed tiles were a specialty. The art of tilemaking was an ancient one, and it survived in Damascus well into the eighteenth century. These tiles—often glazed with indigo, turquoise blue, or

green dyes—were a common sight on floors, walls, and ceilings of buildings, both inside and out. Potters developed new techniques, such as engraving designs on a special coating and then protecting their art with colored transparent glazes. Byzantine

and Italian ceramists would later copy these techniques.

Vases, windows, lamps, drinking glasses, bottles—all sorts of glass objects were created through processes known since ancient times. Arab glassmakers also etched relief designs of animals and arabesques— intricate interlacing patterns of flowers, leaves, or fruit—on their finest pieces. Many mosques and large homes had stunning stained-glass windows with trees, flowers, and geometric patterns in them. Even the borders of the outside walls of these buildings were decorated with shards of colored glass embedded in wet plaster.

New Techniques

Men, goods, and ideas were constantly circulating around the vast empire. For example, a means of manufacturing sturdy, flexible steel weapons was developed in

A Borrowed Secret

The Venetians learned how to make glass from the Arabs. Upon their return to Italy, they kept their discovery a secret. They built glassware workshops on the isolated island of Murano in the Lagoon of Venice. For centuries the Venetians held a monopoly on the manufacture of elegant glassware in the West.

Damascus, Syria. The new technique, called "damasceening," traveled all the way to Spain. New ways of working with leather were developed in Morocco and came to be called "maroquinerie" in French. Techniques that originated in Cordova for the making and repair of shoes were later called "cordonnerie" in France and elsewhere.

Styles and decorative motifs traveled as quickly as manufacturing techniques. Ceramic enamels, fine glassware, and a thin overlay of gold, called gilding, were popular throughout the whole empire. New ways of making soap and of dying fabric spread to the far ends of the Arab world.

LIFE IN THE COUNTRY

The *Book of Land Taxes* advises: "The caliph should be told about discoveries of farmland that might be made fertile through the digging of irrigation ditches. Once the caliph has checked that the report is true, he should give orders for irrigation canals to be dug. The Treasury should pay for this work, and not the landowners."

When new cities such as Baghdad, Raqqa, and Samarra were built, enormous public works projects including the digging of canals were undertaken. In most of the Arab world there was not enough rainfall for crops to grow. Only a hardy wheat, called

durum, and barley grew well; other crops required an additional water supply. Canals, dams, and dykes were built—or often ancient water systems were re-dug—to harness the water in rivers. In Iran and the Maghreb in North Africa, Arabs developed and built underground canals to limit the amount of water lost through evaporation.

Irrigation meant that cultivated farmland produced more abundant crops. In Egypt, 220 pounds (100 kilograms) of sown wheat brought 2,200 pounds (1,000 kilograms) of harvest. In Charlemagne's empire during the same time, 220 pounds of wheat yielded only 440 or 550 pounds (200 or 250 kilograms) of harvest.

New Crops

Sugarcane, rice, bananas, eggplant, artichokes, and spinach originated in the East and slowly traveled westward into Sicily and Spain. Cotton, hemp, linen, and mulberry bushes for silkworms made the same journey. Plants for the production of dyes and perfumes such as indigo, henna, violets, roses, narcissus, and saffron, were grown throughout the Arab world. These fragrant, colorful crops filled entire gardens and fields. Fruit trees such as peach, pear, pomegranate, lemon, and orange were just as abundant. The date palm from lower Iraq became popular in Syria and the Maghreb.

The most treasured flower of all was the rose. Muhammad himself wrote about the beauty of the white rose. The caliph al-Mutawakkil was said to have grown so many varieties of roses in the palace garden that in time, there were no more roses to be found anywhere else in the kingdom!

Agricultural Techniques

Agricultural specialists studied and worked on the selection and improvement of plant and animal species. They refined grafting methods to produce new fruits and flowers. For example, they developed a climbing vine that produced both white and purple grapes, a tree that produced two different kinds of fruit, and a rose that had both red and white petals.

Technicians perfected machines for transporting water, including a waterwheel with buckets, called a *naoura*. Farmers enriched the soil with fertilizers. They also knew how to aerate the land with hoes.

Sleds On Rollers

Special sleds threshed wheat—that is, they remove the grains from the ears. A pair of oxen pulled sleds with wooden cylinders and iron disks around a threshing plate until all the wheat had been separated.

Crossings between rams from the Maghreb and ewes from Spain gave rise to merino sheep, whose wool was very valuable. Arab horse breeders were masterful. The crossbreeds they tested and developed with the North African barb, a strong and fast horse related to the Arabian, produced many of the kinds of horses found in Western Europe today.

Presses

Water, animals, and men powered the millstones that ground olives and stalks of sugarcane.

ANIMALS IN THE MUSLIM WORLD

The author of the ninth century *Book of Animals* listed all the fauna found in the Middle East, making reference to some 350 animals. Over a hundred different books were devoted to the horse alone. These early volumes described different breeds of animals, their characteristics, and their coats. They also explained the techniques of breeding, training, and taming them.

Dromedaries and camels were among the most important of the packsaddle and saddle animals, but donkeys and mules also played a key role in agricultural production. In addition, Arabs raised oxen, buffalo, sheep, goats, and pigeons, whose

droppings were valuable as fertilizer. Pigeon lofts, tall towers made of brick, were scattered throughout the Arab countryside.

Hunting

Hunters tracked partridges, pheasants, moorhens, wild duck, hare, and rabbits. Hunting was both a favorite pastime and a necessary chore. Hunters used falcons and sparrow hawks to help them track wild game. Hunt-

ing manuals showed how to breed and tame these useful birds. When after big game such as gazelles or antelopes, hunters used dogs to help them corner their prey.

When sovereigns went hunting for pleasure, they used grayhounds and cheetahs as well as falcons and hawks. They liked to show proof of their courage and skill by chasing after wildcats and wild boars.

Cavalrymen rode specially trained horses. When they had succeeded in tiring a wild animal, they killed it with spears, swords,

or arrows. Harmless animals such as deer were captured with a lasso.

Animals such as the wildcat were killed because they were a threat to people. Others were hunted for their valuable fur, skin, feathers, or ivory.

The Arabian Horse

This strong and graceful horse was developed to withstand the harsh conditions of the Arabian desert. The Arabian is the forerunner of the thoroughbred.

zoological gardens were opened to the general public.

On the whole, Arabs treated their domestic animals well. The muhtasib punished citizens who overworked or mistreated their animals. They enforced strict rules forbidding cock and ram fights.

Zoological Gardens

Captured wild animals were brought to enrich the palace menagerie and placed on display with other exotic species. The zoological park in Samarra stretched out over a space of 20 square miles (50 square kilometers). In this zoo—as in one in Cairo—lions, elephants, gazelles, giraffes, monkeys, parrots, and many other kinds of animals lived in captivity, separated from one another by canals and cages. On some days, especially on important holidays,

It was common to see dogs lying on the flat rooftops of Arabian homes at night. They were there to guard the house and to warn of approaching danger.

Fishing

Arabs liked to eat fish. Fishermen used nets that were held afloat by cork bobbers to catch a wide variety of fish, including sardines and tuna from the Mediterranean.

ARAB SOCIETY

F arming," said a ninth-century caliph, "has several advantages. First of all, it renders the land fruitful, and thus nourishes all of us. Farming also allows land taxes to be levied and contributes to the public good. It serves trade and enhances our well-being."

In the Golden Age, cultivating land was the most important source of wealth. More than eighty percent of the Arab population lived in the country and lived off the fruits of the land. Unlike farmers working in the West, peasants were not serfs attached to a parcel of land. They were free men. The *ummah,* or community of believers, was made of men who regarded one another as equals. There was no nobility in the Arab world except for the prophet Muhammad and his descendants.

In reality, however, money created a real social hierarchy. Most peasants worked hard to pay heavy taxes that grew considerably more burdensome over time. Peasants who were unable to pay their taxes fled to the city for refuge while the government confiscated all their possessions. Others who chose to borrow money to pay taxes often went broke.

Little by little, large estates began to develop next to properties belonging to the caliph and his family. These estates belonged to dignitaries and high-ranking army officers. Army officers entrusted the management of their lands to administrators called *wakils.*

In the Lap of Luxury

Many Arabs lived a luxurious life-style. The caliph and his court, high-ranking civil servants, military officers, merchants, landowners, and businessmen lived in splendid residences with dozens of rooms, courtyards, and beautiful gardens. They kept many servants. In imitation of princes, they built mosques, public fountains, and caravansaries, and they donated money to char-

Fashion Statements

In ninth-century Baghdad, the caliph's favorite wife set a trend in shoe styles the day she wore a pair of sandals decorated with precious stones. When her rival wore a hairnet covered with jewels to disguise a birthmark on her forehead, this also became the height of fashion.

ity. They surrounded themselves with small courts by welcoming poets, musicians, minstrels, and writers into their homes.

The wives of these fortunate citizens wore clothing cut from silk or brightly colored cloth embroidered with gold. They adorned themselves with pretty jewels and they wore furs during the winter.

Such wealth was evident at mealtime. For example, a famous singer once hosted a dinner for three friends and served no fewer than thirty different poultry dishes. Of course, he also served several other courses and desserts as well.

Privileged Artists

When a famous musician and singer from Baghdad named Ziryab moved to Cordova in 822, the Emir offered him a wealthy country estate and gave him a large monthly allowance. His fortune grew to 30,000 gold

pieces. Whenever he went out he was accompanied by a large retinue of friends on horseback, each of whom was beautifully dressed.

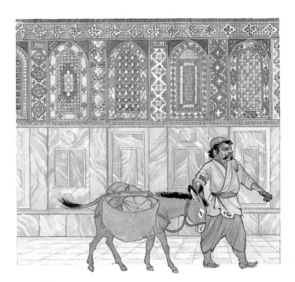

Ziryab the musician was on the cutting edge of fashion and set several new trends in the land of Andalusia (the region of Spain occupied by the Arabs). He recommended that people vary their dress according to the season. For example, he promoted white

clothing in the summer, skins and fur coats in the winter, and silk dresses and brightly colored tunics in the springtime.

Ziryab also taught the inhabitants of Cordova the art of setting a table. He replaced gold and silver goblets with glassware. He also said that the courses of a meal should be served in a specific order. For example, dinners should begin with soup and be followed by meat or poultry, and conclude with sugared treats or cake.

He founded a music conservatory as well as a beauty institute where students were taught how to apply makeup, comb and brush hair, remove unwanted hair, and use toothpaste.

Poor People

People of different regions, ethnic backgrounds, and walks of life rubbed shoulders in crowded city streets every day. Wealth and poverty existed side by side. Clusters of poor people, porters, odd-job men, beggars, and cripples cried out to passersby for coins. After having spent the day wandering city streets, many of these people spent the night sleeping in mosque courtyards.

From time to time riots broke out. Pillaging, arson, and other forms of violence were caused by food shortages, floods, and political or religious movements.

SLAVERY

"Never forget that slaves are your brothers. God has given you the right to own them, but he could just as easily have given them the right to own you," Muhammad told his people.

By the time Islam appeared in the seventh century, in Asia, Europe, and around the Mediterranean Basin enslaved peoples had been regarded as objects to buy or sell for a long time. Very often, their owners exercised the right of life or death over them.

In the Arab world, the slave trade was the domain of non-Muslim "pagans," those people who were considered to be without a true religion. Christians and Jews went to eastern Europe to purchase Slavs, people of slavic descent. This is where our term "slave" came from. Turks from central Asia

Slaves could also buy their own freedom. An owner and a slave agreed on how much the slave would pay over a certain period of time, and the money was then taken out of the slave's earnings.

and blacks from Africa were also bought and sold. And large numbers of children were purchased in the markets of Venice, Kiev, Aachen, and in the Sudan.

Muhammad permitted prisoners of war to be used as slaves. Many foreigners were enslaved in Syria and Iraq during the century or so after his death. But the Prophet also reformed Arab society by passing laws to protect the poor, orphans, women, and slaves. Even though slavery was still accepted, Muhammad encouraged his followers to emancipate, or free, their slaves. The freeing of a slave who had converted to Islam was considered an act of devotion. Because of this encouragement, freed slaves made up a significant part of the empire's population.

Special Schools

Slave owners often put their young slave girls into special schools where they learned how to sing, dance, and recite poetry. These well-educated young women played important roles in the palaces and in the houses of wealthy citizens.

Even after slaves were freed, though, they were still supposed to be loyal to their former owners. Many emancipated slaves were known to have given their own lives to defend the people who had allowed them to be free.

Arab cities were home to many thousands of slaves and enslaved men and women who had been emancipated. Those who remained enslaved were given a certain amount of freedom. They performed many jobs in a wide range of fields such as construction, commerce, and arts and crafts. Some of them even ran their masters' businesses, trading with free men as equals.

dren. The palace of al-Mutawakkil reported that the caliph once received a present of two hundred slaves from one of his generals. This was a common way for governors and generals to express their loyalty to the caliph.

A caliph's household was also sure to include many concubines. Al-Mutawakkil was said to have had 4,000 of them! Young slave women often became their master's concubines. When they gave birth, their children were born free. The mistresses themselves were automatically granted their freedom after their master died. The many unions of this sort led to an extraordinary intermixing of races, creating an empire free of the racial prejudices that have plagued so many of our societies.

Slaves in the army made up a large part of the caliph's personal guard. Slaves could become generals or admirals in the army as well as important royal dignitaries with real power in the royal court.

Slaves in the Royal Palace

The palace was home to thousands of slaves, emancipated slaves, concubines—that is, the mistresses of the caliph—and their chil-

ARAB WOMEN

The wedding day of an Arab woman was a grand occasion. Typically, an enormous party would be held in the middle of the afternoon. Guests would dance merrily to well-known songs played by an all-female orchestra. Servants passed trays of drinks, cakes, and sweets.

The bride would sit upon a throne surrounded by her trousseau and her many wedding presents. A procession came to the house of the bride's father to take her to her new husband's home, which she would never have seen before. There, the party would continue.

Preparing the Wedding

According to Arab tradition, parents, after having consulted with the bride-to-be, were responsible for arranging a marriage contract. The family's first discussion of the marriage took place in the hammam. The groom's mother spoke to the mother of the bride before handing over the negotiations to the two fathers. A contract-signing ceremony in the presence of two witnesses was arranged, and it was decided how much dowry the groom would pay to his future bride. The dowry was usually a symbolic gesture, but it sometimes meant that the groom had to pay a very large sum of money. The amount of the dowry was recorded in the marriage contract by the *qadi* (judge). It was his responsibility to ensure that both the bride and groom were in agreement. This ceremony, so important to the future of the young couple, always concluded with a meal.

The day before the wedding, the bride went to the hammam with the women of her family and her friends to bathe and apply perfume.

On the afternoon of the wedding ceremony, the groom did the same thing with his friends and the men of his family.

The Role of Women

Before the advent of Islam in Arabia, the birth of a baby girl was regarded as a

catastrophe. According to a tradition shared by several ancient cultures, it was acceptable to do away with unwanted newborn girls. The Koran put an end to this slaughter. "Do not kill your children because you fear poverty. We will grant you subsistence to feed them. Killing them would be a

Female Copyists

To earn a living, educated women made copies of the Koran or the books of a library. In the time of the caliphs, in the Arab section of Cordova, there were no less than 170 of these copyists.

terrible mistake," declared the Koran. The Koran also bettered the fate of women by granting them the right to inherit wealth.

In contemporary non-Christian cultures of the Middle East, polygamy was common practice. In other words, a man could have as many wives as he wished. The Koran limited this right by stating that a man could have no more than four wives and that he

had to treat each one of them equally. The Koran set forth some specific rules protecting wives who had been rejected or divorced by their husbands. It also stated that women had to dress decently. Throughout several different periods of history, Muslims have interpreted this council from their holy book to mean that women must wear veils at all times.

Women lived in a separate section of the house called the *harem*, meaning "forbidden." This word also refers to the women who lived there, cooking, cleaning, and raising their children.

Since Muslim men were allowed up to four wives and might have children by all of them, these harems were often quite large. The harem of a royal figure might include not only his wives, but also many mistresses, servants, and female relatives of the ruler. These enormous harems were rare, though, because they were so expensive to keep.

SHARING KNOWLEDGE

Paper was invented by the Chinese in the beginning of the second century. But it was not until the eight century that Chinese prisoners of war revealed the secrets of papermaking to the Arabs. The first paper manufactured in the Arab world was probably made at Samarkand in 751. Other paper mills opened shortly thereafter in Baghdad, Yemen, Syria, Egypt, Spain, and Sicily.

To make paper, rags of linen, hemp, or cotton were plunged into tubs filled with water. Mallets powered by a waterwheel ground the rags until they were transformed into a fibrous, milky substance. Sheets of paper were made by placing this gummy paste on a sieve stretched over a wooden frame. Years later, Arabs brought this technique to Europe.

The spread of paper mills throughout the Arab world led to a tremendous increase in administrative recordkeeping. Paper was also responsible for the widespread distribution of books, knowledge, and culture.

Bookstores

There was a section in every large city where bookstores were easy to find. People who shopped in bookstores were of varied

Papyrus and Parchment

Before the development and spread of paper, all writing was done on papyrus or parchment. Papyrus was made from the leaves of papyrus plants. Parchment was made from the skins of sheep, goats, gazelles, or calves. Parchment made from calves' skin was called vellum.

social backgrounds. Booksellers made lots of money from their trade because most urban residents knew how to read and write. Since reading was popular, there was an impressive number of books to choose from.

Manuscripts sold in bookstores had to be copied by hand. Booksellers often did this slow work themselves, but sometimes they employed male and female scribes to do it for them. Authors often made their living by working as scribes. Their salaries were determined by their intellectual capabilities, the quality of their handwriting,

and their motivation. The better the book was copied, the more it cost.

Specialists traveled the world over looking for new titles to "publish." Some of these specialists hunted down rare manuscripts for collectors. Beautiful editions of rare books were sold at public auctions for very high prices.

Libraries

Princes and wealthy individuals owned their own libraries. Each city had at least one, and sometimes several, public libraries. In the old city of Cairo, the great palace library contained 1.6 million volumes. This library, spread over forty different rooms, was open to the general public. Some visitors to the library stayed to read in one of the great rooms, while others borrowed books and took them home to read. Borrowers were required to give only their

صدق الله العظيم وبلغ رسوله الكريم

name and address. Paper and plumes were available for those who wanted to remain at the library and copy interesting passages.

In some libraries, books were kept locked in bolted closets lining the walls of the room. Lists of the books inside were tacked on the door of each closet. In other libraries, volumes were stored in stacked-up compartments. People wishing to view a book had to look up its title in a catalog and ask a librarian to retrieve it. Sometimes there were several copies of the same manuscript.

Beginning in the tenth century, the spirit of liberty and tolerance that had once characterized the Arab world began to disappear. For example, one dictator who had begun to feel the pressure of fanatical religious movements opposed to such a free flow of knowledge "purged," or cleaned out, the palace library in Cordova. He burned and destroyed everything contained in this unique European institution. Civic trouble and unrest also led to arson and the plundering of palaces and residences—and libraries—belonging to prominent people.

Then, in 1258, the Mongols took Baghdad. These tribes came from the northeastern steppes of Central Asia. Under the strong leadership of Genghis Khan the Mongols expanded, spreading into China, Russia, and Arabia. It was Hülegü, one of Khan's successors, who conquered the city of Baghdad. In the longterm, the Mongol invasion spurred the scholarship, arts, and

political life of the Islamic world. But at first, their invasion physically destroyed much of the Arab empire. The Mongols murdered thousands of scholars. They threw entire libraries into the river and burned any book that they found.

Education

"Search for knowledge, even if you must go to China to find it." This advice given by the prophet Muhammad shows how greatly the Arabs valued learning.

Primary schools were to be found wherever there was a mosque. There were free schools for poor children, so that almost everyone learned how to read and write. Boys and girls attended separate schools.

Aside from reading and writing, schoolchildren studied history, grammar, mathematics, and the Koran. Seated on mats or carpets, they recited and memorized texts written on tablets. Discipline was strict. When a student learned sixty chapters of the Koran, his or her family prepared a large feast at which cakes were served and gifts were offered to the teacher.

It was also an important part of a child's education to learn how to use a bow and arrow and how to swim. A caliph once told the tutor of his sons, "Teach them to swim and accustom them to little sleep."

Advanced Studies

Up until the eleventh century, advanced courses were given by scholars and masters in mosques. Classes were also given among closed circles of acquaintances and friends. Advanced education could last for as long as ten, fifteen, even twenty years. During the course of this continuous program, students went from one master to another and often traveled to new cities when they reached advanced levels in their studies. Large universities attached to mosques were founded in Cairo, Tunis, and Fez.

The First Course

New professors gave their first course in the presence of high-ranking civil servants, masters, scholars, and poets. Speeches celebrating the glory and success of the new teacher were given as a welcome gesture.

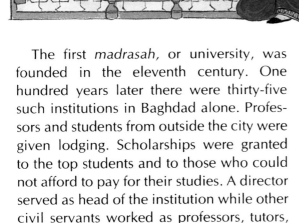

The first *madrasah,* or university, was founded in the eleventh century. One hundred years later there were thirty-five such institutions in Baghdad alone. Professors and students from outside the city were given lodging. Scholarships were granted to the top students and to those who could not afford to pay for their studies. A director served as head of the institution while other civil servants worked as professors, tutors, accountants, and librarians. An imam was named to lead the prayers.

Well-known masters attracted large audiences. They delivered their lectures from a pulpit around which students sat on chairs or benches. At the end of the lecture, students could ask questions orally or by writing them down.

When a professor felt that his student was capable of teaching or of practicing his discipline, he granted him an *ijazah,* or diploma. Some students even received several diplomas from different universities. In Baghdad, an ijazah was required of those wishing to practice medicine.

Special Garb

University professors were appointed by the ruler. The caliph gave each new professor a navy-blue shawl and a black tunic to wear.

SCIENCE

"The ink of the scholar is more sacred than the blood of a martyr," said Muhammad. Muslim missions brought back foreign manuscripts from abroad as early as the eighth century. Ancient Greek, Persian, Indian, and Chinese texts were translated and collected in such places as the House of Wisdom in Baghdad and the Hall of Wisdom in Cairo.

In these institutions, researchers from the far ends of the empire worked to develop new knowledge. Hunain ibn Ishaq, who was in charge of translating works from Greek to Arabic, was also an outstanding physician. He wrote ten books on the eye, creating the earliest known volume of its kind.

These cultural treasures, which were later brought to the West and translated into Latin and other languages, became the basis for philosophical and scientific discovery in the modern world. In fact, the writing of the ancient Greek philosophers Aristotle and Plato first came to Western Europe in Arabic, as did the medical learning of Hippocrates.

Studying the Stars

Ninth-century astronomers had observatories in Baghdad and Damascus. The study of the stars allowed them to determine the direction of Mecca, what times prayers were to be held, and the exact length of the month of Ramadan. The astrolabe, a portable instrument that made it possible to measure the height of the stars in the sky, allowed caravaneers and captains of ships to know exactly where they were. A short while later, the Arab navy brought the concept of the magnetized needle, or compass, back to the Arab empire from China.

Progress in mathematics allowed astronomers to calculate the length of the meridian, the imaginary north-south line on the earth's surface that passes through the poles and determines longitude. In the year 1000 al-Biruni calculated the circumference of the earth and was only 9 miles (15 kilometers) off. This discovery was made several hundred years before Europe admitted that the earth was not flat.

Clever Engineers

A book written in 869 listed no fewer than one hundred inventions, including devices for hot and cold water, mechanical toys, and service elevators. Engineers built countless windmills and watermills on the

banks of rivers. They made water clocks, medical devices, and many automatic devices. For example, they developed an amazing sink equipped with a figurine that

poured water from a jug before handing the user a hand towel and a comb.

A great Andalusian inventor perfected the manufacture of crystal. He produced a "canopy of heaven" with clouds, lightning, and thunder. Because he wanted to fly like a bird, he made a sheath with movable wings out of silk and feathers. One day, he put on this new contraption and jumped off a cliff. He managed to glide for a few minutes before landing safely on the ground.

Arabic Figures

Just try doing a few calculations with Roman figures to see how difficult it is. In Baghdad, during the eighth century, people began using Indian figures. Five centuries later, Europeans began using the same figures and referred to them as "Arabic." This is the ten-digit system of numbers that we use today. It was the Arabs who invented the zero, allowing for representation of very large numbers. Zero was called *sifr,* which means empty.

It was also the Arabs who invented algebra (an Arabic word) and trigonometry. Logarithims were discovered at this time, too.

ARAB MEDICINE

Arab doctors were responsible for developing original and precise medical descriptions. Their knowledge provided the framework upon which European universities would later be modeled.

Arab medical scholars made some very important observations. Abu Bakr al-Razi, known as Rhazes, wrote an enormous medical encyclopedia. He studied infections, such as measles and smallpox, and researched childhood diseases and the influence of psychology on sick patients. He was also the first to use animal gut to stitch

wounds and plaster of Paris to set broken bones.

When choosing a site for a new hospital in Spain, Rhazes hung up raw meat in different parts of town. He said that the hospital should be built at the spot where the least putrified meat hung. He had made a connection between bacteria and infection, something that Europeans would not discover for some time to come.

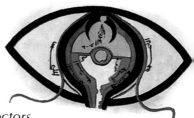

Other Great Doctors

The Muslim Spaniard, Abu al-Qasim, known as Albucasis, summarized everything that was known about surgical methods in the thirtieth volume of his work *The Art of Healing Wounds*. In this important book, he illustrated more than two hundred surgical instruments. He also showed cases where the surgeon's knife was to be used and when false teeth made of bone were recommended.

Ibn Sina, known as Avicenna, was precocious. By the age of ten, he had memorized the Koran. At fourteen, he knew more than all of his knowledgeable masters. At seventeen, he was called to care for the prince of Persia and succeeded in bringing

him back to good health. His two most famous works were an encyclopedia called the *Book of Healing* and the *Canon of Medicine*. His writings were translated into Latin, making him the great master to European physicians from the twelfth to the seventeenth centuries.

Hospitals

Every large city had at least one hospital. At the beginning of the tenth century, Baghdad had at least five of them. Hospitals, which were often housed within the palace, were very modern for their time. Rooms were equipped with comfortable beds. Special areas were reserved for those with contagious diseases, and other zones were designed for those who needed surgery. When a city did not have a separate hospital for women, a section within the public hospital was reserved for them, where all the personnel was female.

Schools of medicine, libraries, pharmacies, mosques, and public baths were attached to each hospital. The administrative staff recorded in logbooks the names of the patients, the care they received, and the food they ate. The cost of medical care was also recorded even though all treatment was free of charge.

Medicines

The study of medicine led to the development of pharmacies. The manuscript of one botanist-pharmacist listed 1,400 "simple" medicines made from single substances such as plants, minerals, or animals. A well-known encyclopedic treatise listed over 760 different drugs.

The first pharmacies opened after the founding of a school of pharmacy. Apothecaries prepared all the potions themselves. In addition to inventing a wide variety of mechanical devices, scholars perfected *al anbik,* or the still, which was used for distilling (creating vapor from liquids). They also discovered acids and *al kohol,* or alcohol. Their research provided key foundations for the study of chemistry.

THE GIFTS OF ISLAM

The Golden Age of the Arabs was a time of tremendous growth in many areas of learning. Much of this knowledge was shared with Medieval Europe. But the simultaneous expansion of the Arabic empire also brought political and religious enemies.

In the eighth century, Charlemagne battled the Arabs in Spain. From the eleventh to the thirteenth centuries, armies of Christians joined in the Crusades to take back Palestine—the Holy Land—from the Muslims. The Mongols invaded from the north. By the thirteenth century the Golden Age was in decline; the empire had begun to crumble.

But the learning and art and many of the traditions born in this time live on. There are about six hundred million followers of Islam of many different races and from a variety of countries in the world today.

DATES TO REMEMBER

570 Birth of Muhammad

612 Muhammad begins to preach the Word of God, the Koran.

622 The Hegira, when Muhammad leaves Mecca for Yathrib (later to be called Medina) and founds the first Arab-Muslim state.

632 Muhammad dies at Medina on June 8th.

The First Four Caliphs (632–661)

632–634 Caliphate of Abu Bakr.

634–644 Caliphate of Umar. The Arabs occupy Syria, Palestine, Mesopotamia (Iraq), Armenia, Persia, Egypt, and Cyrenaica (Libya). They build the towns of Basra, Al-Kufa, Al-Fustat.

644–656 Caliphate of Othman. Official version of the Koran is established.

656–661 Caliphate of Ali. Rise of Khariji and Shiite Muslim sects.

The Umayyad Dynasty (661–750)

661–680 Muawiyah I names his son as his successor, thus founding the first Arab-Muslim dynasty. Damascus, Syria, is the capital of this new dynasty.

670 Founding of Qayrawan in Tunisia.

687–691 Building of the mosque of Umar in Jerusalem.

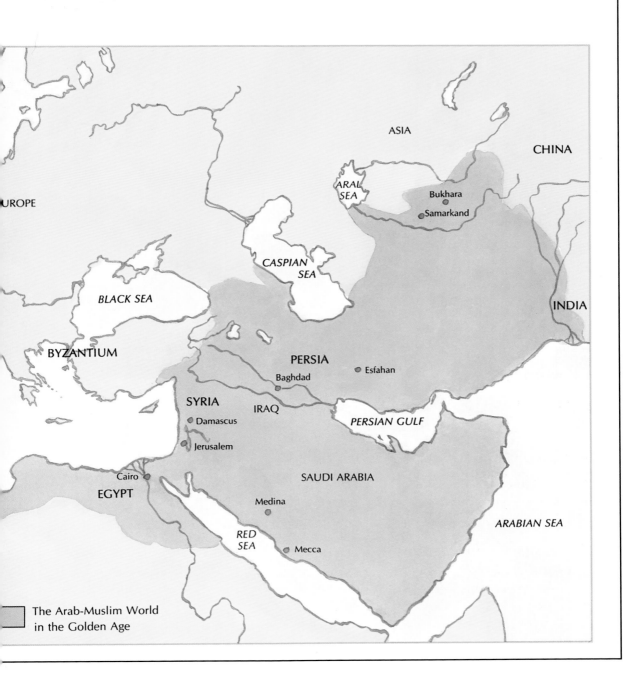

The Arab-Muslim World
in the Golden Age

710 Building of the great mosques in Damascus, Medina, Al-Fustat, Aleppo, and Jerusalem.

711 Muslims conquer Spain and Hindustan in India.

732 Arabs and Franks fight the Battle of Poitiers.

740 Muslims reach the eastern coast of Africa.

The Abbasid Dynasty (750–1258)

750–754 Abu'l-Abbas al-Saffah, first Abbasid caliph, settles in Kufa.

751 Muslims defeat the Chinese in Samarkand in Central Asia.

756 Founding of the Umayyad Emirate in Spain.

762 Baghdad, which later becomes the Abbasid capital, is founded.

786–809 Reign of Harun al-Rashid.

800 Charlemagne is crowned emperor.
The first paper mill is built in Baghdad.
Arab merchants settle in the Cantonese province of China.

831 Arabs settle in Sicily and southern Italy.

836 Samarra is founded.

909 The Fatimid dynasty is founded in Qayrawan.

969 Cairo, Egypt, becomes the capital city of the Fatimid caliphs.

1031 End of the reign of the Umayyads in Spain.

1050 Banu-Hilal nomadic tribes arrive in the Maghreb.

1055 Turkish nomadic tribes called Seljuks arrive in Baghdad.

1056–1147 Almoravid dynasty in the Maghreb.

1060 The Normans (from France) take over Muslim Sicily.

1099 Crusades to Jerusalem.

1130–1269 Almohads succeed the Almoravids.

1236 Cordova is taken by Spanish Christians.

1258 Mongols take Baghdad. End of the Abbasid dynasty.

FIND OUT MORE

Ahsan, M. M. *Muslim Festivals*. Vero Beach, FL: Rourke Corp., 1987.

Hood, Abdul Latif Al. *Islam*. New York: Franklin Watts, 1987.

Keene, Michael. *Looking into Being a Muslim*. London: Batsford England, 1987.

Leacroft, Helen and Richard. *The Buildings of Early Islam*. Reading, Mass.: Addison-Wesley Publishing Co., 1976.

GLOSSARY

Al-Maksoura. The special area in a mosque where the ruler prays.

Bismillah. The opening phrase of the Koran often used in speech and at the beginning of written documents.

Caliph. The ruler of the Islamic empire.

Caliphate. The position held by the caliph.

Caravansary. A trading post.

Hammam. A public steambath.

Harem. The wives and female relatives belonging to one man's household; the place where they lived.

Hegira. Muslim New Year.

Id al-Adha. The holiday in memory of the last day of Muhammad's pilgrimage to Mecca.

Id al-Fitr. The celebration marking the end of Ramadan. See **Ramadan.**

Imam. The person selected to lead public prayers.

Islam. The religion based on revelations to the prophet Muhammad.

Jihad. The striving of the soul to better itself; a holy war to convert others to Islam.

Kaaba. The central monument of the Muslim faith.

Koran. The sacred Muslim text containing the Word of God as spoken through his prophet Muhammad.

Madrasah. An Arab university.

Mawlid. (Also called an-Nabi.) Muhammad's birthday.

Meharist. A soldier who rode a camel.

Mihrab. The alcove of a mosque in the wall closest to Mecca.

Minaret. The tall, slender tower of a mosque.

Mosque. The religious building of the Islamic religion.

Muezzin. The person who announces prayer times.

Muhtasib. The special police chief who guarded the marketplace.

Muslim. A member of the Islamic, or Muslim, faith. See **Islam.**

Naffatun. A flame-throwing military unit.

Qadi. A judge.

Ramadan. One month of fasting to remember the time when the Koran was revealed to Muhammad. The forth pillar of Islam.

Ribat. A small fort with a lookout tower.

Shahada. A formal declaration of Muslim faith. The first of the five pillars of Islam.

Shurtah. The police force.

Suq. A public market.

Ummah. The name for a community of Islamic people.

Vizier. The caliph's closest councilor.

Zakat. The third pillar of the Islamic faith requiring alms-giving.

INDEX